*A* sister is everything special to your heart... and the dearest friend you'll ever have

Barbara J. Hall

**Blue Mountain Arts**®
*Other titles in this series...*

*Daughters*

*Friendship*

*Love*

*Mothers*

*Sons*

A Blue Mountain Arts® Collection
to Share with a Sister
Who Means So Much

Edited by Gwendolyn Gray

**Blue Mountain Press**™

Boulder, Colorado

Library of Congress Control Number: 2003099550
ISBN: 0-88396-837-1

Certain trademarks are used under license.
BLUE MOUNTAIN PRESS is registered in U.S. Patent and Trademark Office.

Manufactured in Thailand.
First Printing: 2004

 This book is printed on recycled paper.

# Blue Mountain Arts, Inc.

P.O. Box 4549, Boulder, Colorado 80306

# Contents

(Authors listed in order of first appearance)

# In a Sister's Heart

Sisters are two young women who have been brought up together. And they dearly love one another... with all the tenderness of their hearts and a union that is so very strong.

George Sand

*S*isters come in all shapes and sizes ~ small and tall, thick and thin ~ but it isn't the packaging that makes you my beloved sister ~ it's because you are the best, and I love you with all my heart.

Sandra Fubini

# Sisters

Sisters fill the heart with laughter.
Sisters listen and never say
   "I told you so."
Sisters share all that
   they have to give.
Sisters are always there
   when you need them.
Sisters are wonderful friends
   throughout the years.
Sisters are shoulders to lean on
   when your strength is low.
Sisters know you better than
   you know yourself.
Sisters share memories
   that no one else knows.
Sisters are always appreciated
   and forever loved.
Sisters are wonderful gifts
   that last a lifetime.

❧ Donna Gephart

# Sisters Carry Each Other
## in Their Hearts
## Forever and Always

Whether they live near each other or far apart, sisters walk through life together. They're there for each other no matter what... sharing everything.

Sisters are connected at the heart and in their blood, and their loyalty to one another is permanent. No one can ever break that bond. They don't give up on each other easily. They have the utmost sensitivity and compassion for one another because they were born into the same family.

Sisters aren't afraid to break rules for each other. They defend each other; they take chances for each other. They've cried together and laughed together. They know each other's secrets. They forgive each other when they make mistakes, and they can almost read each other's mind.

Sisters teach each other lessons as they stand by each other in life, and they are there for each other through everything that matters.

No one can ever take the place of a sister. Thank you for being mine. I carry you in my heart forever and always.

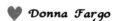 Donna Fargo

We share something that is stronger than any storm, that is wonderful and caring and warm, that is supportive and trusting and sweet. Our love is something our hearts and our happiness will always treasure and keep.

Anna Tafoya

# Having a Sister like You Is One of the Sweetest Joys of My Entire Life

There are many blessings to count in this world: good things and special people who keep smiles on my face. I have a few friends who are wonderful to me. I have people I can talk to and trust, and I have relations whose common bonds will always be interwoven with love and togetherness.

But as radiant and as wondrous as even the very best people can be, none of them could ever begin to take your place in my heart. That precious space will always belong to you alone.

 Douglas Pagels

# There Is So Much That Is So Precious Between Us...

The love that exists between us is like a very rare and beautiful flower. It's there, no matter what. It weathers the storms, it bends in the breeze, it blossoms in every season of the year, and it stays near me everywhere I go.

The sharing that exists between us is like a foundation in my life. Upon it, I have built so many feelings and shared so many experiences with you. I have counted on our sharing for strength ~ and I have never been disappointed. I have relied on it for security, and I have found more reassurance than my words can say.

So often I find myself depending on the bond between us ~ because it has been the basis for a special trust that I share with you alone.

The happiness that exists between us is like a gift, one that seems to have been given to me to make sure that my heart would always be full and my memories would always be beautiful. I have discovered that the loving combination of family ties and precious friendship that you and I share is ~ and always will be ~ a treasure I cherish and a dream come true.

Just between you and me, Sister...
I love you a lot, and I don't know what I'd ever do without you.

♥ Laurel Atherton

# Sister Wishes

One of my heart's favorite hopes is that the happiness you give away will come back to warm you each and every day of your life.

Sydney Nealson

# These Are the Gifts
# I Wish for You...

Happiness. Deep down within.
Serenity. With each sunrise.
Success. In each facet of your life.
Close and caring friends.
Love. That never ends.

Special memories. Of all the yesterdays.
A bright today. With much to
    be thankful for.
A path. That leads to beautiful tomorrows.

Dreams. That do their best to come true.
And appreciation. Of all the wonderful
    things about you.

❦ Collin McCarty

*I* want these things to be our "sister wishes." *And I* want them to do everything they can to keep coming true for us all our lives...

*That* we may always be more than close.
*That* nothing will ever come between
   the bond of love we're blessed with.
*That* we will celebrate our similarities,
   honor the things that make each of
   us unique, and quietly realize that
   every part of the circle of our lives
   is a special, precious gift.

*That I* will always be here for you,
   as you will be for me.
*That* we will listen with love.

That we will share everything that
   wants to ~ and needs to ~ be shared.
That we will care unconditionally.

That we will trust so much, and we will
   talk things out.
That we will nurture each other's
   spirit and warm each other's soul.
That even when no one else knows
   what's going on inside...
   you and I will gently understand.

And that wherever you go, you will be
   in my heart, and my hand
      will be in your hand.

♥ Katie Russell

*My* brightest hope and most precious wish is that you know, without a doubt, just how important you are to me and how often you bring the sweetest smile to my day.

Jane Andrews

# Ten Wishes for You, My Sister

1. I wish you confidence: when things get tough, when you're overwhelmed, when you think of giving up

2. I wish you patience: with your own trials and temptations, and with others

3. I wish you an adjustable attitude: one that doesn't react, but responds with well-thought-out actions and feelings

4. I wish you beauty: within yourself, in your surroundings, and in nature

5. I wish you excitement: new things to enjoy and learn and experience

6. I wish you fun: laughter and smiles any way you can get them

7. I wish you companionship: people to share your happiness and sorrows, your troubles and joys

8. I wish you health: mental, physical, and emotional

9. I wish you peace: with others, yourself, and in your environment

10. I wish you love: pure, unconditional, and eternal

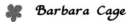 Barbara Cage

$\mathcal{A}$ sister like you is a special gift...
We like to do so many of
the same things, and we share
a lot of wonderful, fun moments.
You respect me for my strengths,
as I admire you for yours.
We encourage each other
during our difficult times,
and laugh with each other
during our good times.
I know I can be myself with you.

A sister like you is a precious gift...
We can tell each other
our secret dreams and desires.

We can cheer each other on to
success and happiness,
and wipe each other's tears
when we are sad and disappointed.
You are a bright light in my life,
and you have a special place in my heart.

I want to wish you all your best
dreams come true,
and that you have success and joy,
a fulfilled heart, and laughter.
And I want to tell you that
you are beautiful to me,
and I cherish our friendship.

♥ Donna Levine Small

# No Friend like a Sister

*F*or there is no friend like a sister
In calm or stormy weather:
To cheer one on the tedious way,
To fetch one if one goes astray,
To lift one if one totters down,
To strengthen whilst one stands.

Christina Rossetti

# Sisters Are Forever Friends

Each morning
when the day begins,
when other friendships
fade or end,
sisters are forever.
Seasons come
and seasons go.
Summer rains
turn into snow.
But no matter
where you live
or how far you go...
sisters are forever.

❧ Ashley Rice

*A* sister is friendship, fun, and family
all rolled up into one beautiful person
She's everything special to your heart
the one to lift your spirits
and the dearest friend
you'll ever have

# You'll Always Be My Best Friend

Sister, I have come to realize that
somewhere between our
childhood and adult years,
You became not only a friend to
me, but a best friend ~
A friend who will always be there
for me with strength and encouragement
And with continuous love and support.
You're a friend who knows me
better than anyone else
And accepts me unconditionally
for who I am ~
A friend whose personality leaves me smiling
time and time again
And whose presence in my life brings
such joyful blessings to me.
You're a friend who knows with
certainty that, even with our
differences, our closeness will
forever bond our hearts as the
best of friends.
I love you, and I treasure you ~
both as a sister and as a friend!

 Susan Hickman Sater

# Our "Friendship Quilt"

We share a relationship
   that is unique and rare and wonderful.

The yesterdays of our lives are
threaded together like a friendship quilt,
reflecting on scenes we each know so well
and which today live on in some of
   our most beautiful memories.

We have a certain something between us
that has so many special elements to it,
elements that make it different
from any other kind of love.

It has friendship added to family,
perspective added to an interwoven past,
and more honest communication than
almost any two people can share.

Nicest of all, maybe... is that the
relationship between us is quilted with
a love that never leaves, with listening
and laughing, with comfort and trust,
and with the sweet and special knowledge
that we will always care.

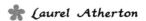 Laurel Atherton

# I Am Honored to Call You My Sister, and Fortunate to Call You My Friend

I know that I can trust you
with my most cherished treasures,
with my heart and soul, and
with every secret I hold.
I know that you will listen
without criticizing me for my mistakes.
You hear what I am trying to say,
even when I fail to express myself clearly.
I know that I can believe you
without worrying
that you will mislead me,
because you are honest with me
even when honesty means disagreement.

I know that you will accept me,
despite every wrong turn I've taken
and every bad decision I've made.
You simply love who I am.
I know that our hearts are connected
on the deepest level.
You know me so well;
your insight and your view of me
make me feel complete.
I know that I am special
because you are so special.
I'm proud of our friendship and
the strength we have together.
I am honored to call you my sister
and fortunate to call you my friend.

♥ Regina Hill

# The Support of a Sister

There can be no situation in life in which the conversation of my dear sister will not administer some comfort to me.

Lady Mary Wortley Montagu

*Sister, I want to remind you of how unique our relationship is and to tell you that you could never, ever be replaced in my life.*

*I want to let you know how much I appreciate you. I want to thank you for every time you have shared a worry or tear, every time you have listened and been the only one who understood, and every time you were there when I had nowhere else to turn.*

*I want to assure you that our relationship is one of the most important in my life, and that you are not only my sister, but a dear and cherished friend.*

 *Barbara Cage*

*A* sister is a hand within yours, enfolded with love and understanding. She gives you a feeling that makes you wonder what you would ever do without her, and no one is loved so dearly.

Carey Martin

# You Are the One Person Who Really Understands Me

I'm pretty sure I would lose my mind
if I didn't have you for my sister.
No one understands me like you do.
No one else laughs
   at quite the same things that I do.
No one can comfort me
in the same way that you comfort me.
No one else can give me confidence
and reasons to believe in myself
   like you do.

You keep me grounded.
You remind me of who I am
and where I've been.
You bring so much fun
and so many happy times to my life.
I don't know what I'd do without you.

♥ Jane Andrews

# My Sister Is...

someone who helps me find my smile.
Who accepts me for what I am. Who lets
me know that my efforts really are
worthwhile, and that my accomplishments
are worthy ones. She lets me know that
she will catch me if I fall. She's so much
more wonderful than she will admit to
being. She watches out for me and helps
me through it all.

## My Sister Is...

someone I'm very proud to be related to.
Having her as such a special part of my
family has given me memories that I
wouldn't trade for anything ~ and hopes
that I'll have for as long as I live. Even
if there are times when the two of us are
far away from each other, our thoughts
will make sure we stay together.

## My Sister Is...

a person who is great to have around. She's someone who laughs at my jokes (maybe because she has the same warped sense of humor!), and she understands the times when I need a shoulder to cry on. She is there for me in the exact same way that I will always be there for her. Our friendship will always remain, and our love will never depart.

## My Sister...

deserves to know that even though I don't always get a chance to show it, she is absolutely essential to the happiness... that lives within my heart.

❀ Ann Turrel

*T*here is no one I'd rather laugh or cry with or share my innermost thoughts with, and there is absolutely no one I'd rather have as my sister.

Barbara Cage

# I'm So Lucky You Are My Sister

There aren't many people I can share my thoughts with, and fewer still that would understand them if I tried. There aren't many people that will listen to the same story over and over and continue to enjoy it just because I do. There aren't many people that will laugh at an old joke with me because the memory of telling it is funnier than the joke ever was.

There aren't many people who know me inside and out and love me despite it all, but then there aren't many people that I would be as happy to have for a sister as you.

♥ Melissa Merriman

# A Special Kind of Bond

> *A*re we not like two volumes of one book?
>
> Marceline Desbordes~Valmore

*I* feel so blessed to share secrets,
uncontrollable laughter, tears,
and challenges with you.
*You* have been there for me
  whenever *I* needed a favor;
you help me sort out my feelings.
We have faced dreams together ~
holding on to each other
when they've come true
and watching as others have faded away.
*Together* we are a mighty force,
united in a way most people aren't.
We are fiercely protective and proud
  of each other,
yet not against pointing out
  a fault or two when we need to.
*Honesty* has always been important
in our relationship, and so has love.
*I* cherish our closeness
and *I* want you to know how much
*I* love and appreciate you.

 Barbara Cage

*You* know full as well as
I do the value of sisters'
affection to each other;
there is nothing like it on
this earth.

Charlotte Brontë

As *Sisters*,
we have a special bond that
can't be broken by time,
distance, or the *Inconveniences* of
life. We share secrets, hopes,
dreams, and fantasies that no one
else knows ~ *Sometimes* with
laughter, sometimes through tears,
always with love ~ just because
we're sisters. *That* means we
can disagree about the smallest things
or be serious rivals, but it
doesn't last. *Even* talking
badly about each other is allowed;
as sisters, we get that
privilege on very *Rare* occasions ~
certain that nothing and no one
can ever really come between
us. *You See*, nothing is
more important than being sisters, and...
no sister is more important
than you!

♥ *Andrea L. Hines*

*There's* a bridge between your heart and mine. *The* laughter, secrets, tears, hopes, dreams, love, and memories we've shared have caused our lives to be forever intertwined.

Jason Blume

# You Mean So Much to Me

You are a wonderful constant in my life,
like the sun that rises and sets each day.
I can count on your love and support
   like no other.
The sounds of your laughter
   and your voice on the phone
are comfortable reminders
   of our lives together ~
like a tree planted long ago
which has grown from a seedling
   into a source of shade.
When it rains, you are like my umbrella,
forever there to protect me,
and when it's sunny, you are there to rejoice
in the light of love that ties us.
Like a best friend, you love me
   without judgment ~
and you listen with patience
   and understanding.
I am so happy that you are,
and will always be...
                    My Sister.

                          Ellen M. DuBois

# A Sister's Love Is a Bond That Lasts Forever

A sister's love is a special gift of close family ties ~ woven in the fabric of shared experiences, with memories of people and events that mean so much to both of you...

The bond of love you share with a sister is strengthened by all the fond recollections of milestones in your lives. It is as unbreakable as the courage she has given you when you faced challenges together.

A sister's love is playful and fun. It holds echoes of her laughter from childhood. It is as faithful as her friendship. You can depend on her for so much. You can expect her to listen to you and understand feelings that other people cannot fathom.

You can trust that she will help you with no strings attached. You can expect her to be there for you and care about you like only a sister can.

A sister's love is a gift of acceptance that allows you to be yourself always. It is the sweet peace of being with someone whose presence alone conveys how dear you are to her. Her love cheers for you when you experience success. It sheds tears with you when you are hurting inside.

A sister's love shines with pride in you. It holds you tight day and night, and never outgrows its closeness to you. It is a priceless gift because it comes from her heart.

♥ Jacqueline Schiff

# ACKNOWLEDGMENTS

We gratefully acknowledge the permission granted by the following authors, publishers, and authors' representatives to reprint poems or excerpts from their publications.

Barbara J. Hall for "A sister is friendship, fun, and family...." Copyright © 2004 by Barbara J. Hall. All rights reserved.

Donna Gephart for "Sisters." Copyright © 2004 by Donna Gephart. All rights reserved.

PrimaDonna Entertainment Corp. for "Sisters Carry Each Other in Their Hearts Forever and Always" by Donna Fargo. Copyright © 2002 by PrimaDonna Entertainment Corp. All rights reserved.

Susan Hickman Sater for "You'll Always Be My Best Friend." Copyright © 2004 by Susan Hickman Sater. All rights reserved.

Melissa Merriman for "I'm So Lucky You Are My Sister." Copyright © 2004 by Melissa Merriman. All rights reserved.

Jason Blume for "There's a bridge between...." Copyright © 2004 by Jason Blume. All rights reserved.

Ellen M. DuBois for "You Mean So Much to Me." Copyright © 2004 by Ellen M. DuBois. All rights reserved.

Jacqueline Schiff for "A Sister's Love Is a Bond That Lasts Forever." Copyright © 2004 by Jacqueline Schiff. All rights reserved.

A careful effort has been made to trace the ownership of selections used in this anthology in order to obtain permission to reprint copyrighted material and give proper credit to the copyright owners. If any error or omission has occurred, it is completely inadvertent, and we would like to make corrections in future editions provided that written notification is made to the publisher:

BLUE MOUNTAIN ARTS, INC., P.O. Box 4549, Boulder, Colorado 80306.